This journal belongs to

OPEN like a flower to the song of life and the magic that surrounds and flows through all. Acknowledge, reaffirm, understand and celebrate your connection with Gaia.

This journal holds sacred space. It is free of judgement and dogma and is blossoming with a loving invitation to liberate, release and express all you are meant to be. The messengers you find within are your trusted companions. Speak with them, for they will show you the way ...

Greet these pages with hope, daring, honesty and curiosity and relish in all you wish to create, and all you dream of becoming.

Ravynne

I AM GAIA. I am the daughter of Great Spirit, who is the Source of All. I am both magical and divine, as is all I create. I am the Great Mother. I am your mother, and you, beautiful soul, are a physical manifestation of my love.

I speak to you in visions, exposing your senses to the glory and mystery of the world that surrounds you. I offer you wisdom and guidance, so that you may know and understand both yourself and this world in which you dwell, so that you may see and embrace the divine in both yourself and in nature.

I send to you my children and protectors — the faeries, the creatures of the animal kingdom and of nature and dragonkind. They speak on my behalf. They are my messengers and their words are a gift from me to you.

Our one shared desire is to help guide you on your journey, to open you to the shining beauty and power of your soul and shadow, to the awareness that you are not alone, and to tell you that you are loved.

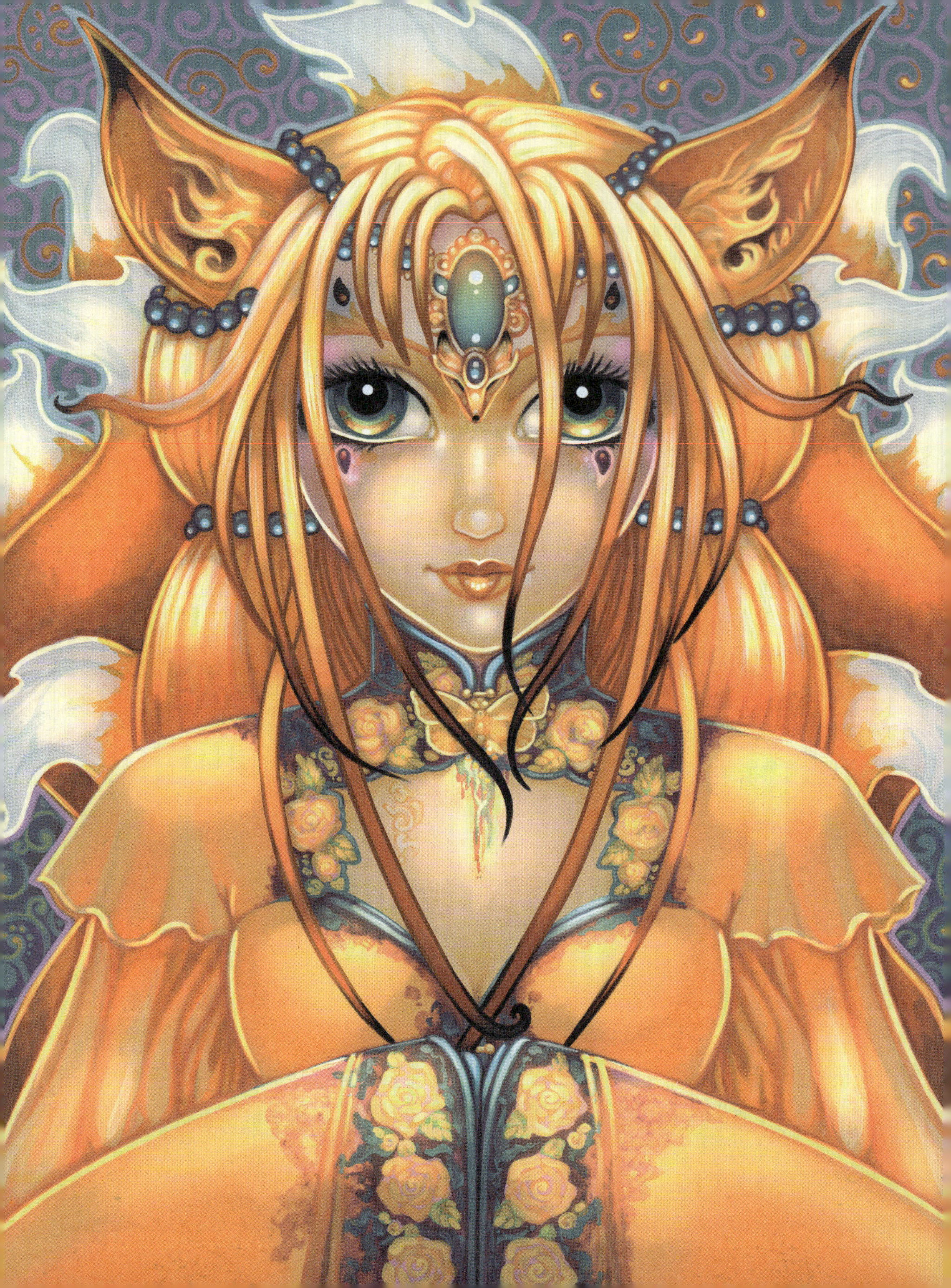

Ravynne Phelan

AS A CHILD, Ravynne was told a career in art was an unattainable dream. Made vulnerable by her neurodivergence, she believed this to be truth and laid down her brushes. For the next fourteen years, she lived in a world of grey, empty of colour, dreams and goals until she was officially diagnosed with depression and introduced to art as a form of emotional release and therapy. Thus, her dreams of colour were rekindled.

Some dreams are more than dreams — they are destiny. And, Ravynne was fated to become an artist and share her message of magic, healing and self-empowerment. However, destiny does not ensure an easy road. After several years as a commercial illustrator, Ravynne began to feel an emptiness once more. After much soul-searching, she realised her creativity was meant to have a more spiritual message. Dedicating herself to Great Spirit and Gaia, Ravynne turned her back on her career as a fantasy book-cover artist and children's book illustrator, first to illustrate, and then to write, oracle and tarot cards as well as journals and colouring books.

Today, Ravynne is an internationally recognised and bestselling creator. Her titles include *A Seeker's Tale Journal, Messenger Oracle, Divinity Journal, The Dreamer's Story Tarot Journal, Dreams of Dragons & Dragon Kin Coloring Book, Seek Writing & Creativity Journal, I Am Writing & Creativity Journal, Dreams of Magic,* and the award-winning *Dreams of Gaia Tarot, Dreams of Gaia Tarot Pocket Edition, Ravynne Phelan's Spirit Animal Coloring Book* and *Seeker Oracle.*